Other books in this series:
Thank Heavens for Friends   To my Grandmother with Love
For Mother, a Gift of Love   Marriage a Keepsake
Love a Celebration   Words of Comfort
To my Daughter with Love

EDITED BY HELEN EXLEY
BORDER ILLUSTRATIONS BY SHARON BASSIN

I would like to dedicate this book to my dad, Tor, and to Richard,
my husband, father of my boys – you are the kindest dad I have
ever seen – never forget that.
My thanks go to Margaret Montgomery and Jane Varley who
rescued the book when it was running late. And also to Pam
Brown, who trudged around countless libraries to find father
poems for me and then herself wrote some of the best pieces
in the book.

The border artwork is dedicated to Sharon Bassin's father, Harry.

Published simultaneously in 1994 by Exley Publications in
Great Britain, and Exley Giftbooks in the USA.

12   11   10   9   8   7   6   5   4   3

Picture and text selection by © Helen Exley 1994.
Border Illustrations © Sharon Bassin 1994.
Picture research by Image Select International.
Typeset by Delta, Watford.
Printed in China.

Exley Publications Ltd, 16 Chalk Hill, Watford,
Herts WD1 4BN, United Kingdom.
Exley Publications LLC, 232 Madison Avenue,
Suite 1206, NY 10016, USA.

For my FATHER

A Helen Exley Giftbook

EXLEY
NEW YORK • WATFORD, UK

Abstracted from home, I know no happiness in this world.

THOMAS JEFFERSON

If I were asked to name the world's greatest need, I should say unhesitatingly; wise mothers and . . . exemplary fathers.

DAVID O. McKAY

Fatherhood precipitates many men into a desperate scramble to grow up over night.

Dads either know too little about the subject on which you have to write an essay – or far, far, *far* too much.

We are finally grown up when we can forgive our parents.

You worship him as a hero, then despise him as a man. Eventually you love him as a human being.

It's easy, when your child believes you are always right, to slip into believing it's the truth.

PAM BROWN

If you live without being a father you will die without being a human being.

We think of a father as an old, or at least a middle-aged man. The astounding truth is that most fathers are young men, and that they make their greatest sacrifices in their youth. I never meet a young man in a public park on Sunday morning wheeling his first baby without feeling an ache of reverence.

JAMES DOUGLAS

No man can possibly know what life means, what the world means, what anything means, until he has a child and loves it. And then the whole universe changes and nothing will ever again seem exactly as it seemed before.

LAFCADIO HEARN

One word of command from me is obeyed by millions . . . but I cannot get my three daughters, Pamela, Felicity and Joan, to come down to breakfast on time.

VISCOUNT ARCHIBALD WAVELL

The first service a child does his father is to make him foolish.

ENGLISH PROVERB

Last night my child was born – a very strong boy, with large black eyes. . . If you ever become a father, I think the strangest and strongest sensation of your life will be hearing for the first time the thin cry of your own child. For a moment you have the strange feeling of being double; but there is something more, quite impossible to analyze – perhaps the echo in a man's heart of all the sensations felt by all the fathers and mothers of his race at a similar instant in the past. It is a very tender, but also a very ghostly feeling.

Lafcadio Hearn

When one becomes a father, then first one becomes a son. Standing by the crib of one's own baby, with that world-old pang of compassion and protectiveness toward this so little creature that has all its course to run, the heart flies back in yearning and gratitude to those who felt just so towards one's self. Then for the first time one understands the homely succession of sacrifices and pains by which life is transmitted and fostered down the stumbling generations of men.

CHRISTOPHER MORLEY

TO CREATE A CHILD

Out of love for the tangible, the visible, the
    present,
I have called the unknown;
Out of the understood,
mystery.
Now she is flesh, nothing is adequate.
This moment has set her beyond her mother's
knowing,
beyond my comprehension.
She is far more than we conceived.
With her first breath she absorbed the world,
with her first cry she accepted death.
She is the heart of another universe.

All I can do I will;
Shelter her,
teach her,
love her,
learn each day something of what she is.

But never again in utter confidence.
Never again unafraid.
She, in her vulnerability,
reveals the dangers of the dark.

PETER GRAY

In the Service of the Empress

My wife and I, we entered domestic service five weeks ago. It is much as we expected it would be. We spend much of our time in the kitchen now, muttering in the way of servants whenever an intermission occurs between the imperious yells.

Like most dictators, our employer seems to find it difficult distinguishing between day and night. She sleeps in the day but then in the small hours or at dawn the summons comes, just as Hitler's and Stalin's came, to send feet clattering across the halls of serpentine and syenite.

But so far we have been spared the monologues about the New Order. New Orders do not interest her, for she has gone back beyond all ordered society to a state of egomania that not even dictators know. One blue eye opens, and there must be food; it shuts, and there must be warmth. If either is lacking, all hell breaks loose.

As servants, we are out of the reach of any trade union. We have gone back, too, beyond serfdom and slavery, to the wood and the moon. However much we mutter, we know we are in the service of a living god and there is nothing we can do about it. When last measured the god was 22 inches long.

BYRON ROGERS

The final judge of every man is his child.

PAM BROWN

What a father says to his children is not heard by the world, but it will be heard by posterity.

JEAN PAUL RICHTER

What do I owe my father? Everything.

HENRY VAN DYKE

You see that boy of mine? Though but five, he governs the universe. Yes, for he rules his mother, his mother rules me, I rule Athens, and Athens the world.

THEMISTOCLES

He is the happiest, be he king or peasant, who finds peace in his home.

JOHANN WOLFGANG VON GOETHE

When bairns are young they gar their parents' head ache; When they are auld they make their hearts ache.

SCOTTISH PROVERB

THE JUDGE

Say of him what you please, but I know my child's failings.

I do not love him because he is good, but because
he is my little child.

How should you know how dear he can be when you try to weigh his merits against his faults?

When I must punish him, he becomes all the more a part of my being.

When I cause his tears to come, my heart weeps with him.

I alone have a right to blame and punish, for he only may chastise who loves.

RABINDRANATH TAGORE

. . . For who knows what my girl will be? She's only a few months old, and a surprise already – and I imagine I've just got a lot more surprises coming. But in the end, I suppose, I just want to give her love and the assurance of a home on earth. This child was not born merely to extend my ego, nor even to give me unbroken pleasure, nor to provide me with a plaything to be fussed over, neglected, shown off and then put away. She was born that I might give her a first foot in this world and might help her to want to live in it. She is here through me, and I am responsible for her – and I'm not looking for any escape-clauses there. Having a child alters the rights of every man, and I don't expect to live as I did without her. I am hers to be with, and hope to be what she needs, and know of no reason why I should ever desert her.

LAURIE LEE

A FATHER'S HAPPINESS

To show a child what has once delighted you, to find the child's delight added to your own, so that there is now a double delight seen in the glow of trust and affection, this is happiness.

J. B. PRIESTLEY

NICER THAN HUMANS

Children are corks
Exploding suddenly during heat-waves;
Hosepipes gone mad
Spraying us with cold water;
Going off behind our backs
Like rip-raps
They assault our world with clowning.

They are tough as whipcord
And as easily swayed
As gossamer, lightly hurt
As dandelion clocks;
Repetitious as pod-peas;
Maddening as flies;
Direct as nudity;
Unhinged as moths at night yet wise
As old roads and buried tracks can be;
They seem to belong
To an earlier species,
Imbued with the fragility of pure spirit
In bodies of india-rubber.

We have no defence
Against their wiles,
Innocent faces, ice-cream smiles;
As Milligan said
In a goonish quip,
So much nicer than human beings!

JOHN BARRON MAYS

THE FATHER'S SONG

Great snowslide,
Stay away from my igloo,
I have my four children and my wife;
They can never enrich you.

Strong snowslide,
Roll past my weak house.
There sleep my dear ones in the world.
Snowslide, let their night be calm.

Sinister snowslide,
I just built an igloo here, sheltered from the
    wind.
It is my fault if it is put wrong.
Snowslide, hear me from your mountain.

Greedy snowslide,
There is enough to smash and smother.
Fall down over the ice,
Bury stones and cliffs and rocks.

Snowslide, I own so little in the world.
Keep away from my igloo, stop not our travels.
Nothing will you gain by our horror and death,
Mighty snowslide, mighty snowslide.

Little snowslide,
Four children and my wife are my whole world,
   all I own,
All I can lose, nothing can you gain.
Snowslide, save my house, stay on your summit.

ESKIMO PRAYER

TO MY DAUGHTER

Bright clasp of her whole hand around my
    finger,
My daughter, as we walk together now.
All my life I'll feel a ring invisibly
Circle this bone with shining: when she is
    grown
Far from today as her eyes are far already.

STEPHEN SPENDER

Only a father would ride on the rollercoaster with me, come off with a green face and say he had a good time.

LONI CASALE, AGE 11

A father is for being talked into being a butterfly in my school play.

ROBIN ROSENBALM, AGE 11

A dad is a person that thinks he knows everything but doesn't even understand simple new math.

MELISSA WELLINGTON, AGE 10

A father is a person that puts things off so he can put them off next week again.

JIMMY ATHENS, AGE 11

I like my dad, because when I was five he would play football. But now he can't play football, because he's thirty.

THERON CARNELL, AGE 9

A father is the type of person who says he is eating all of your birthday chocolates so you won't get fillings in your teeth.

LESLIE ROLES, AGE 13

Sometimes when he gets mad at me I can understand why.

MICHELLE WALSH, AGE 13

A dad is somebody who can get away with doing things he tells you not to do.

PAUL RAICHE, AGE 14

I was born because I wanted to be like my dad.

SAMUEL LIN

GIRL'S-EYE VIEW OF RELATIVES

The thing to remember about fathers is, they're
    men.
A girl has to keep it in mind.
They are dragon-seekers, bent on improbable
    rescues.
Scratch any father, you find
Someone chock-full of qualms and romantic
    terrors,
Believing change is a threat –
Like your first shoes with heels on, like your
    first bicycle
It took such months to get.

Walk in strange woods, they warn you about the
    snakes there.
Climb, and they fear you'll fall.
Books, angular boys, or swimming in deep
    water –
Fathers mistrust them all.
Men are the worriers. It is difficult for them
To learn what they must learn:
How you have a journey to take and very likely,
For a while, will not return.

PHYLLIS McGINLEY

THE THINGS MY CHILDREN TAUGHT ME

One of the best things about children is their humanizing influence. You have to deal with them on their level. You cannot impress them with your title or your prestige or your bluster. You cannot hide from them. You have to relate to them directly as people, and that is something many of us don't do very often. Talk about reducing life to simplicities! Trying to communicate with a child is one of the simplest acts imaginable. Just the two of you. When it's not driving you crazy ("Why?" "Because. . .") it can be wonderfully refreshing.

Most of all, children teach the capacity for enjoyment. The ecstasy a child can find in a carrot or an apple is simply amazing. They like to run just for the fun of it, or stick their heads out the window of the car to feel the wind. They can break through all those levels of control, all those accretions of detachment and sobriety that plug up your laugh ducts. When I come home at night and the two of them burst through the door, running down the walk to greet me, the world is a beautiful place. No matter what else has happened, it's beautiful.

When you are really in love, you think you are the first person who has ever felt that way. Parenthood should be the same way. I don't care if it's trite – I love to hear my children laugh, just as I love to see my wife standing in the doorway, watching us.

STEVEN V. ROBERTS

IN PRAISE OF FATHERS

In the baby lies the future of the world. Mother must hold the baby close so that the baby knows it is his world but father must take him to the highest hill so that he can see what his world is like.

A MAYAN INDIAN PROVERB

FATHER SAYS

Father says
Never
let
me
see
you
doing
that
again
father says
tell you once
tell you a thousand times
come hell or high water
his finger drills my shoulder
never let me see you doing that again

My brother knows all his phrases off by heart
so we practice them in bed at night.

MICHAEL ROSEN

FOR A FATHER

With the exact length and pace of his father's
    stride
The son walks,
Echoes and intonations of his father's speech
Are heard when he talks.

Once when the table was tall,
And the chair a wood
He absorbed his father's smile and carefully
    copied
The way he stood.

He grew into exile slowly,
With pride and remorse,
In some way better than his begetters,
In others worse.

And now having chosen, with strangers,
Half glad of his choice,
He smiles with his father's hesitant smile
And speaks with his voice.

ANTHONY CRONIN

As she has grown as a daughter, so have I grown as a father, and have learned to bury away my wishful images of her, to watch her take charge of her own directions....

True, in the beginning she showed certain promising tendrils – early soppiness about the moon, an especially fine touch on the piano, and an unquestioning belief in my faultlessness. But these shoots withered soon; she never quite finished her first-year Mozart, began to find the moon-rise a bit of a bore, and though ready to be guided by me on her choice of chocolate bars, gradually came to the conclusion, as her eyes grew level with mine, that I was really a bit of a joke.

So what I've got in the place of my early self-indulgencies is not the compliant doll of an old dad's fantasy, but a glowing girl with a dazzling and complicated personality, one with immense energy in the pursuit of happiness and despair, who expresses her love for me, not in secret half-smiles, or in an intimate sharing of silences, but in noisy shouts, happy punches, and hungry burying of teeth in my ear-lobes.

Certainly she is no daddy's soft shadow, nor ever will be; she exists on a different scale to my first fond imaginings. She is at last herself....

Not at all what I planned, or what I expected, but I don't think I would exchange her for anything else.

"Jessy", by Laurie Lee

A father sees a son nearing manhood.
What shall he tell that son?
"Life is hard; be steel; be a rock."
And this might stand him for the storms
and serve him for humdrum and monotony
and guide him amid sudden betrayals
and tighten him for slack moments.
"Life is a soft loam; be gentle; go easy."
And this too might serve him.
Brutes have been gentled where lashes failed.
The growth of a frail flower in a path up
has sometimes shattered and split a rock.
A tough will counts. So does desire.
So does a rich soft wanting.
Without rich wanting nothing arrives.
Tell him too much money has killed men
and left them dead years before burial:
the quest of lucre beyond a few easy needs
has twisted good enough men
sometimes into dry thwarted worms.
Tell him time as a stuff can be wasted.
Tell him to be a fool every so often
and to have no shame over having been a fool
yet learning something out of every folly
hoping to repeat none of the cheap follies
thus arriving at intimate understanding
of a world numbering many fools.

Tell him to be alone often and get at himself
and above all tell himself no lies about himself
whatever the white lies and protective fronts
he may use amongst other people.
Tell him solitude is creative if he is strong
and the final decisions are made in silent rooms.
Tell him to be different from other people
if it comes natural and easy being different.
Let him have lazy days seeking his deeper motives.
Let him seek deep for where his is a born natural.
  Then he may understand Shakespeare
  and the Wright brothers, Pasteur, Pavlov,
  Michael Faraday and free imaginations
bringing changes into a world resenting change.
  He will be lonely enough to have time for the
  work he knows as his own.

CARL SANDBURG

APOLOGY

"Sorry" seems inadequate.
"I never meant it", fatuous.
And it's too late for tears.
How then to tell you all I've learned these
    twenty years?
I stand here in the cold December day
and thrust a gift-wrapped parcel
    at your chest
and say
"Best love from all of us.
A happy birthday, Dad."

A box of time remembered.

The same late gift you gave your father once
. . . and he to his.

PAM BROWN

At twenty he had put on this costume of fatherhood, padded the shoulders, added to his height, deepened his voice to fit the part. I never saw the greasepaint or the wig line as I clasped his hand.

Only when I had grown and had come to know everything myself, did I see the fraud. A well-intentioned man, but not the man I thought him. A little man. A man who blurred into the small suburban landscape, his friends as nondescript and kind as he, his work respectable, ambition long since burned away. I saw him so till now, but suddenly I find him changed. Years and indifference have made him careless. He forsook the padding and the heels somewhere along the way, but how could this diminish his reality? He is, I see, himself. Not shrunken, but the man he was before we came. His voice has lifted. His eyes are more alert, no longer speaking of preoccupations with children's shoes and adolescent brushes with the Law.

He has taken up again the things we interrupted, the skills we crowded to the edges of his life. He is no longer obliged to steal time for himself. We are his companions now, his friends, rather than demanding voices always at his elbow.

He has not grown young again. I see now that he was never old. The painted wrinkles that he still retains, the careful silver streaks, no longer fool us. My dad's a man as young as any of his children.

Perhaps a little younger.

CHARLOTTE GRAY

BEFORE IT GETS TOO LATE, DAD

Poets are inclined to weep
when their papas are buried deep,
tucked up and out of sight.
They wallow in complete recall,
which doesn't help their dads at all,
or make the wrong things right.
But I'm no poet, so I'll say
all my apologies today
for every teenage fight,
for every laziness and lie,
for every bitterness and sigh
I caused you.... Better live than write,
old love; we'll use our days
in daft, companionable ways
while we've still life and light.

PAM BROWN

MY FATHER

I took my father for granted,
never thought him courageous,
A clean watchful man
who never raised his voice;
never stood at a barricade
but quietly held his course.
Never unjust to the young,
never betrayed his trust.
Secret in his love.

Now I know
the small disciplines of day by day,
spoke for a valiant heart.

HENRY CHAPIN

One moment's obedience to natural law and an ordinary man finds himself called upon to be wise, kindly, patient, loving, dispenser of justice, arbiter of truth, consultant paediatrician, expert in education, financial wizard, mender of toys, source of all knowledge, master of skills.

And to wake one day to find that he has failed and that he is, after all, a silly old devil who's out of touch and out of date. He should not be discouraged. He will eventually be reinstated.

PETER GRAY

STANZAS FOR MY DAUGHTER

Tell her I love
   she will remember me
always, for she
is of love's graces made;
   she will remember
these streets where the moon's shade
falls and my shadow mingles
with shadows sprung
from a midnight tree.

Tell her I love that I
am neither in cloud nor sky,
stone nor cloud,
but only this
walled garden she knows well
and which her body is.

Her eyes alone shall make
me blossom for her sake;
contained within her, all
my days shall flower or die,
birthday or funeral
concealed where no man's eye
finds me unless she says
He is my flesh and I
am what he was.

HORACE GREGORY

FATHER

Your coughing hurts me more. On winter mornings
And coming up the road it is your sign.
I see at last that you are growing old.
This summer you retired. Whose life with mine
Was mingled for so long and never noticed
More than as the flavour of a coat
Smelling of tobacco, as a forehead
Frowning at the desk-top where you wrote
Figures in a black book, adding up
To everything, to nothing, to a wage –
I whose youth so took your love for granted,
What answer can I make now to your age?

Father, it is too late. I want for you
All the chances that were never yours,
Summer. . . but what can come? Only the summer
That autumn brings, the days warm for five hours
After the mist clears, and before the sunset.
Father, then I want for you no less.
Here in the autumn garden where you sit
Unlearning slowly an old restlessness,
Red admirals still tremble on the stonecrop,
While swallows come, as to a meeting-place.
Read now, remember, watch your children's children,
And fall asleep with sunlight on your face.

DAVID SUTTON

Acknowledgements: The publisher gratefully acknowledge permission to reproduce copyright material. Every effort has been made to trace copyright holders, but in a few cases this has proved impossible. The publishers ould be interested to hear from any copyright holders not here acknowledged.
PAM BROWN, "Apology" and "Before it gets too late, Dad", © Pam Brown 1985; HENRY CHAPIN, "My Father" from *The Haunt of Time*, William L. Bauhan Publisher, Dublin, N.H. (USA), 1981; ANTHONY CRONIN, "For a Father" from *New and Selected Poems*, published by Carcanet Press Ltd. © 1982 Anthony Cronin; PETER FREUCHEN (translator) "The fathers song" from *Book of the Eskimos*. Reprinted by permission of Don Congden Associates; HORACE GREGORY, "Stanzas for my daughter" from *Collected Poems* copyright © 1964 by Horace Gregory. Reprinted by permission of Harold Matson Company, Inc.; LAURIE LEE "The Firstborn" from *I Can't Stay Long*. Reproduced by permission of Penguin Books Ltd.; PHYLLIS McGINLEY, "Girls-Eye iew of Relatives", from *Times Three*. Copyright © 1959 by Phyllis McGinley. Originally published in the New Yorker. Reprinted by permission of Viking Penguin Inc., New York and Martin Secker and Warburg Limited; CHRISTOPHER MORLEY, excerpt from "Mince Pie". Copyright 1919 by Christopher Morley. Copyright renewed 1947 by Christopher Morley. Reprinted by permission of HarperCollins Publishers Inc.; STEPHEN V. ROBERTS, "The things my children taught me" from *Confessions of a Confirmed Father*, originally published in Redbook Magazine. BYRON ROGERS, extract from "In the service of the empress", first published in The Sunday Times 18th September 1983. Copyright © Times Newspapers Ltd. 1993; MICHAEL ROSEN "Father says" by permission of Scholastic Publications Ltd. CARL SANDBURG, "Nearing manhood" from *The People, Yes* by Carl Sandburg, copyright 1936 by Harcourt Brace Jovanovich, Inc., renewed 1964 by Carl Sandburg; STEPHEN SPENDER "To my Daughter" from *Collected Poems*. Reprinted by permission of the Peters Fraser & Dunlop Group Ltd.; DAVID SUTTON, "Fathers" from *Absences and Celebrations*. Reprinted by permission of Chatto and Windus.
Picture Credits: Archiv Für Kunst und Geschichte: pages 5, 6, 9, 13, 21, 24-5, 45, 48, 55, 58, 60; Bridgeman Art Library: cover; © 1997 Peter Szumowski, "Sundays", private collection, pages 17, 27, 31, 37, 51, 52, 57; Chris Beetles: page 22; Christies Colour Library: pages 15, 34, 47, 52; Dresden, Gemaldegalerie, Neue Meister: page 5; Fine Art Photographic Limited: page 43; Fondazione Contini Bonacossi Firenze: page 18; Galerie George, London: page 37; Giraudon: pages 31, 51; Galleria Statale Tretjakov, Mosca: page 39; © DACS 1994 Liebermann, Max "Schusterwerkstatt", 1881, page 9; Louvre, Paris: page 31; © DACS 1994 Wolfgang Matthever, "Im Kahn", 1970, pages 24-5; Moskva, Tretjakow, Galerie: page 21, 39; Museo Civico Piacenza: page 11; Musee Des Beaux-Arts, Tournai: page 51; Musee d'Orsay, Paris: page 45; Nationalgalerie, Berlin: page 9; Prag, Narodni Galerie: page 55; Rona Gallery, London: page 57; Scala: pages 11, 18, 39; Staaliches Museum, Schwein: pages 24-5; © Jean Stockdale, 1994 "Roses Day at Churchfield; Towneley Hall Art Gallery & Museum: page 27; © L. A. Tessler, 1994 Max Liebermann "Dune und Meer", 1909 Kunstsallon, Koln: page 58.